THE CYCLIST'S CODEX

Protocols for Pedalling in Pelotons, Preserving a
Pulse, Pushing Power, Pootling on Paths, and
Not Being a Prat on the Road

THE CYCLIST'S CODEX: PROTOCOLS FOR PEDALLING IN PELOTONS,
PRESERVING A PULSE, PUSHING POWER, POOTLING ON PATHS, AND NOT
BEING A PRAT ON THE ROAD

Published in the United Kingdom 2025
by SIMPLY SAID LTD

Hardback ISBN 978-0-9954643-3-9
Version 1.1 (MT Zefal)

CONTENTS

WARM-UP

In the beginning, there was the Wheel. And the Wheel was good.

The Wheel begat the Frame, the Frame begat the Chain, and lo, the Gears turned. And in the fullness of time, Man rode forth upon Carbon and Aluminium (and occasionally Steel, which he claimed was "more honest") and declared: "Let us form a Group Ride, that we may be both swift and sociable." And there was much rejoicing.

…Until, inevitably, someone sprinted for a café sign, unannounced, mid-conversation, and didn't even wait for the others to catch up.

Thus, dear reader, began the slow, painful birth of the Cyclist's Codex.

Welcome to *The Cyclist's Codex: Protocols for Pedalling in Pelotons, Preserving a Pulse, Pushing Power, Pootling on Paths, and Not Being a Prat on the Road*.

This is not just a book.

It is scripture.

It is statute.

It is a long-overdue act of legislative intervention for the woefully lawless realm of recreational and semi-serious group cycling.

This Warm-Up, like all warm-ups, is to be taken seriously–though not *too* seriously. The experienced rider will know that all good rides begin with a gentle spin and an unnecessarily officious discussion about the route.

So too does this book.

Consider what follows your metaphorical ten minutes at 60% FTP while someone in arm warmers insists on explaining what "tempo" really means.

WHY THIS EXISTS

Because you, noble cyclist, need guidance. Not you specifically, of course. You're perfect. You're measured, punctual, appropriately attired, and you know exactly when to take your turn on the front and when to shut up and sit in. This book is not for you.

It's for the others.

The half-wheelers.

The unannounced "I'm doing a session" surgers.

The over-fuelled, under-washed zealots who think a café stop is a competitive event.

The emoji-abusers in the WhatsApp group who message "Still on?" at 7:58am for an 8:00am departure.

The self-proclaimed "not that fit at the moment" riders who proceed to treat every incline as a solo time trial.

The ones who don't signal. The ones who don't wave.

The ones who think "no drop" is a legally non-binding suggestion.

This guide exists for them. And for all of us who have suffered under their rule of chaos.

It also exists because, like it or not, cycling—particularly group cycling—is a game of unspoken rules. The problem is that no one has spoken them.

Until now.

This book is the Grand Codification of what has, for too long, been left to passive aggression, silent judgment, or the post-ride sofa questioning, "What was that all about?"

This, friends, is the sacred law of the road.

WHAT LIES AHEAD

The Codex is divided, not unlike a club ride on a steep hill, into chapters. Each addresses a critical domain in which etiquette must triumph over ego, or else the peloton perishes.

You will find chapters with clauses, and sub clauses on:

MEETING ARRANGEMENTS: Because time waits for no man, and neither should a group ride. If you're late, the group is not rude. You are.

DRESS CODE: A careful examination of the sock-height clause, the subtleties of kit allegiance, and the severe penalties for flappy jackets.

WHATSAPP GOVERNANCE: How to communicate clearly without descending into GIFs, guilt trips, or group mutinies.

PACK RIDING: An ancient art governed by geometry, physics, and the unspoken agreement not to surge every thirty seconds.

WEATHER PROTOCOLS: Rain is not a war crime. You are not made of sugar. Nor is wind except above recognised thresholds. Harden up, bring a rain jacket or at least smash yourself on Zwift.

CAFÉ STOPS: Civilisation's last true forum. A test of patience, pastry paying politics, and how much grunting is acceptable and encouraged upon ride recommencement.

FUELLING AND FEEDING: Less a nutrition guide, more a reminder to bring something so you don't bonk.

CLIMBING & RE-GROUPING: The joy of flexing uphill and the moral obligation to wait at the summit and pretend you're also tired.

DESCENDING: A sacred trust. If you don't know your limits, you're not brave—you're a liability.

SAFETY AND SIGNALS: You are part of a unit. Point out holes. Announce cars. Or be held liable in the court of opinion.

MECHANICAL MISCONDUCT: Tubes, tools, chains, and the shame of the ill-maintained drivetrain.

INCLUSIVITY AND INDUCTION: What to do when a friend-of-a-friend turns up with no idea what "rolling through" means.

POST-RIDE CONDUCT: The etiquette of Strava uploads, debriefing etiquette, and the unwritten rule that if you didn't give kudos, you weren't really there.

Each chapter is written in the appropriate tone: judicial, exasperated, sometimes theological.

Because what you are entering into—this act of shared suffering, coordinated effort, and caffeine-dependant diplomacy—is not just a ride. It is a ritual.

On Strength and Service

Let it be said plainly: some of you are stronger. This is not a flaw. It is your cross to bear. You will take longer pulls. You will close gaps. You will do so with grace, without comment, and without repeatedly reminding us how little you've been training. On climbs, go ahead and stretch your legs. Dance like Contador. Suffer theatrically. But at the summit, you wait. You regroup. You do not roll on "just to keep warm." You wait, like a decent human being with a working Garmin and a soul.

What This Is Not

This is not a training manual. It will not make you faster. In fact, if followed correctly, it may slow you down slightly, as you wait for a mechanical, give someone else the prime seat at the café, or hold off pushing down that 2% downhill with a tailwind.

Nor is this a book about racing, training zones, VO2 max, marginal gains, or chainring size. You will find only one graphic. This is a book about being bearable. Enjoyable, even. It's about the human side of cycling—the unspoken social code that separates cyclists from the triathletes.

FINAL WORDS BEFORE THE GUN GOES

If you finish this book and still believe you don't need rules—then congratulations, you are officially *that* person. But for the rest of us—those who love the camaraderie, the rhythm, the quiet joy of rolling two-by-two into the sunrise with mates who know how to call out "car back" and mean it—this Codex is our compact.

Clip in.

Read on.

And for the love of Coppi, don't half-wheel.

MAMIL'S HIERARCHY OF NEEDS

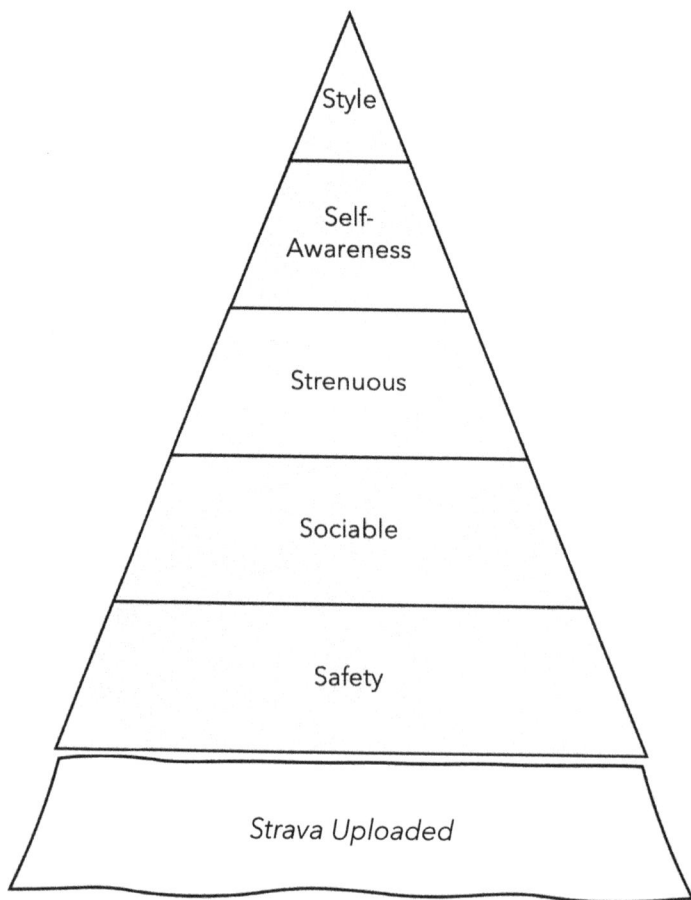

Style

Self-Awareness

Strenuous

Sociable

Safety

Strava Uploaded

As revealed to the faithful through miles, mishaps, and mid-ride meltdowns.
A sacred pyramid of purpose—climbed in cleats, powered by caffeine, and founded, inevitably, on the gospel of Strava.

0. STRAVA UPLOAD (THE WIFI OF THE WHEEL)

Let us begin where all rides begin: with digital validation. Before nutrition, before safety, before friendships—there is Strava. If you didn't record it, it didn't happen. If your device failed, you failed. You may have avoided every pothole and held every wheel like a surgeon in a wind tunnel, but without a GPS trace, you are invisible. Forgotten. Unkudosed. A wraith in Lycra.

This is not vanity. It is your *digital immortality*. The climb is hard. The legs are tired. But those KOMs won't hold themselves.

RIDER SYMPTOMS:

- Refuses to start moving until the Garmin confirms satellites.

- Rides 400m past home to round up the distance.

- Deletes and restarts a ride if auto-pause was left on.

- Knows every segment within a 20km radius by heart, yet claims not to care.

1. SAFETY (THE HELMET OF ENLIGHTENMENT)

Once Strava is rolling, the next priority is *not dying*. This includes avoiding others' wheels, potholes, and death-by-roundabout. Safety is not a vibe; it's a duty of care to those around you. It's knowing that your unpredictable bunny hop for "fun"or pocket grab could take out six people and ruin someone's season (and their front fork).

Point out hazards. Ride in straight lines. Use hand signals, not interpretive dance. Assume no one knows what they're doing and be pleasantly surprised when someone does.

RIDER SYMPTOMS:

- Wears a helmet without needing to be told by the UCI.
- Knows how to fix a puncture in less than two YouTube videos' worth of time.
- Shouts "CLEAR!" like a battlefield medic at every junction.

2. SOCIABILITY (THE PACT OF THE PELOTON)

Congratulations. You are upright and uploading. Now comes the real test: being *bearable*. Group cycling is a fragile ecosystem of shared effort, juggling family timetables and unspoken etiquette. Blow through a junction, surge on every hill, or fail to acknowledge the café queue and you've breached the social contract.

Sociability means looking out for others, calling out hazards *and* good pastries, and not treating every moment as a race simulation. It's understanding that riding as a group requires more than just a common speed—it demands a common *spirit*.

RIDER SYMPTOMS:

- Waits for the dropped without moral grandstanding.

- Checks on stranded cyclists, "You got everything you need?"

- Knows when to talk, when to be silent, and when to lie ("You're looking strong").

- Buys a round of coffees without documenting it.

3. STRENUOUSNESS (THE ART OF SUFFERING WELL)

Once safe and sociable, your primal need to *feel something* rears its watt-hungry head. Cycling, at its core, is the ritual of voluntary suffering. You're not just here for coffee and camaraderie—you came to *work*. To sweat. To chase personal glory in the unspoken sprint for the town sign while pretending it was "just a stretch of the legs."

This is where lungs burn, thighs bark, and dignity gets tested on 14% ramps while trying to look casual. You could back off. But that would be… what's the word… sensible?

RIDER SYMPTOMS:

- Calls a 3-hour ride "recovery."

- Disguises fatigue by opening legs and looking at chain.

- Declares "steady pace" but clips out with salt streaks and empty gels.

- Feigns surprise when a social ride turns tactical.

4. SELF-AWARENESS (THE INTERNAL POWER METER)

You are now strong. But are you wise?

Self-awareness is the ability to read a group as deftly as you read a gradient. It's knowing your efforts affect others. It's recognising that your FTP is not a personality. And that shouting "hold the wheel!" at someone cramping is not inspirational—it's just bullying in cleats.

This level is about restraint. Timing. Emotional intelligence on two wheels. You may be fit, but if no one wants to ride with you, what's the point?

RIDER SYMPTOMS:

- Understands that strength ≠ leadership.
- Takes longer pulls without saying, "I'll just do a bit more."
- Soft-pedals so the group can regroup.
- Can sense 1% drop in biomechanical efficiency and falls back to offer a gel!

5. STYLE (THE FINAL ASCENT)

At the top of the pyramid lies the most elusive virtue: *Style*. Not fashion. Not expensive kit. True style is effortless excellence. It's moving in unison with your group. Clipping in clean. Waving at cars that didn't kill you. Looking good because you're riding well, not because you're colour-matched to your bidons.

Style is the apex where safety, strength, and social grace blend into one seamless dance. It's riding hard without riding over others. It's appearing as though you float, even when you're quietly dying inside.

RIDER SYMPTOMS:

- Kit fits. Socks match. Mudguards are aligned.
- Descends like a whisper and climbs like a sermon.
- Comes out for a ride, even when CBA, but prevent Dave from riding solo.

- Doesn't post about "morning vibes"–*is* the morning vibe.

- Somehow always has just the right thing to say, or nothing at all.

Climb well. Fail often. And may your ride be uploaded before your legs realise what you've done.

THE CODEX CITATION SCALE (CCS)

The Codes Citation Scale (CSS)

A 7-point progressive scale of transgression and social consequence, adapted for use within all honourable cycling groups.

This scale allows for swift, appropriate punishment of breaches against the sacred rites of the peloton. Use liberally. Enforce without remorse.

CCS 1 - *The Glance*

PUNISHMENT: A subtle look. One eyebrow may rise. Perhaps a soft exhale through the nose. Nothing is said, but you feel it in your soul.
EFFECT: Self-doubt activated. You'll replay the moment all afternoon.

CCS 2 - *The Group Reminder*

PUNISHMENT: Someone says, "Just a reminder for everyone…" while looking directly at you.
EFFECT: Public correction, thinly veiled as a friendly note. Others nod. You curl up inside.

CCS 3 - *The Café Tax*

PUNISHMENT: You buy coffee, cake, and cover oat milk upgrades for the entire group next ride.
EFFECT: Financial penance. Public acknowledgment of guilt. Everyone enjoys their food slightly more.

CCS 4 - *The Tribunal*

PUNISHMENT: A post-ride group debrief is held. You are the main topic. The word "pattern" is used.
EFFECT: Ego dismantled via polite discussion and

long pauses. Apologies expected. Silence afterwards deafening.

CCS 5 - *The Banter Blackout*

PUNISHMENT: You are removed from all memes, ride chat, and midweek GIFs. Total social blackout.
EFFECT: No kudos. No notifications. You become a shadow, haunting the group with unacknowledged ride uploads.

CCS 6 - *The Ejection*

PUNISHMENT: Immediate removal from the WhatsApp group. No warning. Reinstatement process unclear and humiliating.
EFFECT: Social death. Rebuilding trust requires café reparations, public grovelling, and a multi-ride probation period.

CCS 7 - *External Escalation*

PUNISHMENT: Incident referred to police, paramedics, or local cycling authority. Possibly immortalised in helmet-cam footage titled *"Idiot Cyclist Causes Carnage."*
EFFECT: Legal or medical involvement. Ride reviewed as "the one we don't talk about."

NOTE: Riders may receive compounded citations. For example, repeated CCS 2 infractions may automatically trigger CCS 4. Abuse of the scale is itself a CCS 1 offence.

CHAPTER 1: THE IMMUTABLE LAW OF THE MEETING POINT

Where two or more riders are gathered in the name of the ride, punctuality shall be their covenant.

§1.0 – STATUTORY ARRIVAL

1.1.0 The Agreed Time is Sacred
All riders shall arrive on site, dressed, clipped, and mentally ready at or before the published departure time (hereafter referred to as T0).
– Riders arriving at T0+1min shall be met with stony silence and a thinly veiled sigh.
– Riders arriving after T0+3min without prior notification shall be issued a **CCS 2: Group Reminder**, typically phrased as "We were just talking about punctuality actually."

1.2.0 Fashionably Late is Not a Recognised Clause
All arguments citing traffic, domestic drama, missing gloves, or existential dread shall be acknowledged politely and summarily ignored.
– Repeat offenders shall be marked in the group ledger and rotated to coffee-paying status (see Chapter 6: The Café Taxation Protocols).
– Clause 1.2.1: The "On My Way" Defence - Messages sent at or after T0 saying "leaving now" are considered admissions of guilt.

1.3.0 Pre-Notification of Delay
In the event of genuine hindrance (mechanical, parental, divine), a rider may notify the group via WhatsApp no later than T0–10min.
– This triggers Clause 1.3.1: Conditional Mercy, in which the group may elect to wait, mock, or proceed depending on historical behaviour and mood.

1.4.0 The Wait Window (Locally Negotiable Clause)
Groups may establish a maximum wait window (e.g. 5

minutes post-T0), after which The Ride Shall Depart.
– The Left-Behind shall receive no sympathy, only a
digital thumbs-up and a link to the route.
– This clause may be negotiated once per season,
preferably during an AGM or group curry.

§1.2.0 – PARKING PROTOCOLS AND FAFF CONTAINMENT

1.2.1 The Five-Minute Faff Limit
Upon arrival, riders shall be granted a maximum of 5
minutes to conduct final checks: tyre squeeze, bidon
rattle, headunit interrogation, and mirror pose
assessment.
– Riders exceeding this faff window shall be moved
to the outer circle and required to conduct remaining
operations under social pressure.

1.2.2 Forgotten Pump is a Mortal Sin
The sin of arriving sans pump shall be punished with
immediate public ridicule.
– Three-time offenders shall be issued **CCS 3: The
Café Tax**, for crimes against preparedness.
– Clause 1.2.2.1: The "Can I Borrow a Tube?"
Reoffence Protocol triggers automatic escalation to
CCS 4: The Tribunal.

1.2.3 Assembly Protocol and Vehicle Contingency
Clause
1.2.3.1 All riders shall, wherever feasible, arrive at the
designated meeting point by bicycle, thereby
demonstrating commitment, punctuality, and
mechanical readiness.
– Riders arriving by bike shall occupy space
respectfully, avoid straddling the entrance, and not

loiter mid-thoroughfare under the false belief that they are the centre of the universe.

1.2.3.2 Riders arriving by motor vehicle (hereafter referred to as vehicular adjuncts) must observe the following sub-clauses:
(a) Park considerately—not across driveways, pubs, cycle paths, or near wedding venues
(b) Avoid urinating in public sightlines, especially not upon post boxes, commemorative benches, or heritage signage
(c) Do not claim "it fits" when reversing a Qashqai into a space meant for a Brompton
– Clause 1.2.3.2.1: Reverse parking into designated pre-ride conversational clusters shall result in exclusion from warm-up banter, and may prompt a passive **CCS 2: Group Reminder** about social awareness.
– Clause 1.2.3.2.2: Loud music, open car doors flapping like a sales forecourt, or full kit assembly from a car boot over a 12-minute period shall trigger **CCS 1: The Glance**, escalating to **CCS 3: Café Tax** if overshoes are involved before breakfast.

§1.3.0 – THE PRE-RIDE RITUAL
1.3.1 Acknowledgement of Fellow Riders
All participants shall greet one another with a nod, verbal acknowledgement, fist bump or appropriate seasonal pleasantry.
– Failure to do so may result in silent treatment and assignment to the back of the line during crosswinds.

1.3.2 Route Briefing (Optional Clause)

If a route briefing is conducted, it shall be short, factual, and not delivered as a TED talk.

– Riders who insist on "just one more tweak to the GPX file" shall be fined with audible yawns and a possible **CCS 2**.

1.3.3 Late Arrivals Catching Up

No group shall be morally obligated to soft-pedal for riders who couldn't be bothered to leave on time.

– Exceptions apply only if the late party brings baked goods or confesses their sins publicly during the café stop.

§1.4.0 - ENFORCEMENT AND RECOURSE

1.4.1 Citation Protocols

Any breach of §1.0-§1.3.3 may trigger an immediate Citation from the appointed Ride Captain, or, in their absence, the most punctual rider present.

– All citations must be issued with exaggerated courtesy and legalistic flourish.

1.4.2 Appeals Process

Appeals may be submitted in writing, within 24 hours, to the group WhatsApp, but will be ignored unless they're funny.

– Riders citing childcare, severe weather, or existential crises must include supporting memes.

§1.5.0 - LOCAL CUSTOMISATION PROVISIONS

1.5.1 Group-Defined Wait Window

Each group shall agree on a fixed maximum waiting time after T0 for late arrivals–typically 5 minutes

unless otherwise stated.
– Clause 1.5.1.1: Groups may opt to extend the wait window in winter (e.g. up to 10 minutes) but must communicate this clearly in pre-ride chat, not halfway through a croissant.

1.5.2 Route Briefing Addenda
The route lead may add the following to the standard briefing without triggering CCS:
(a) Estimated café arrival time (within ±10 mins),
(b) Specific mentions of unpaved surfaces—particularly if "gravel" means "tractor path,"
(c) Clear end-point information, including where the beers are and if showers exist.

1.5.3 Repeal of Mercy for Habitual Latecomers
If lateness is endemic, Clause 1.3.1 (Conditional Mercy) may be suspended.
– In such groups, any rider arriving after T0 without prior warning shall be met, not with sympathy, but with **CCS 3: Café Tax**, and will buy the first round at the stop without protest.

1.5.4 Designated Car Park Conduct Area
Groups where many riders drive to the start may mark a "Kit Assembly Zone" in the car park to contain the faff.
– Riders spreading kit across multiple spaces, drying shoes on the roof, or changing shorts in public shall trigger **CCS 1: The Glance**.
– Overshoes may not be fitted until you've had at least one spoken interaction.

CHAPTER 2: DRESS CODE AND LIVERY COMPLIANCE

And the Lord of the Road did say: "Let thy garments be worthy, tight-fitting, and free from shameful flappage."

§2.1 - SOCK HEIGHT DOCTRINE

2.1.1 Socks shall rise above the malleolus (ankle bone) but below the gastrocnemius (calf muscle), forming what is henceforth designated The Zone of Acceptable Compression.
– Lengths outside this zone are classed as "barely there" or "tube sock travesty," both punishable by **CCS 1: THE GLANCE** and aggressive side-eye.
– Clause 2.1.1a: *White Sock Sanctity* - White socks are elevated to semi-sacred status during dry weather. Muddy conditions suspend this ruling under the "Practical Mercy Provision."

§2.2 - LYCRA INTEGRITY AND AERODYNAMIC RESPECTABILITY

2.2.1 Jerseys shall be form-fitting, zipped at least ¾ up unless engaged in climbing, and free from flapping in the wind like heretical bunting.
2.2.2 Gilets and jackets shall be assessed on both function and auditory disruption. If your windbreaker sounds like a tent in a gale, it is in violation.
– Flapping beyond acceptable thresholds shall result in **CCS 2**.
– Clause 2.2.2a: *The Commuter Exemption* - High-vis and baggy kit are granted conditional immunity if accompanied by mudguards, panniers, and visible despair.

§2.3 - CLUB KIT REGULATIONS

2.3.1 The wearing of official club kit constitutes a declaration of representation. Any rider intending to

wear such regalia must notify the group at least 12 hours in advance.
– This shall allow others to don matching kit or refuse to ride out of spite.
– Clause 2.3.1a: Wearing club kit from a rival club is punishable by **CCS 3: CAFÉ TAX**, and must be followed by a public explanation and potential kit-burning ceremony.

2.3.2 Riders shall not wear pro team kit unless:
(a) They are, or were, a member of said team,
(b) They received the kit as a gift directly from the rider,
(c) They are under 16.
– Failure to comply shall trigger **CCS 4: TRIBUNAL**, with public interrogation and historical wattage review.

§2.4 – COLOUR COORDINATION AND THE MAD MIX MANDATE

2.4.1 Kit shall follow a recognisable colour scheme. Riders may not resemble a packet of highlighters, nor display more than three major colour zones unless sanctioned by Carnival Law.
– Contraveners will receive **CCS 2**, and may be forcibly photographed for future ridicule.
– Clause 2.4.1a: The *"Just Grabbed Whatever" Defence* is admissible only once per season.

§2.5 – SHORTS, GLOVES, AND SEASONAL PROTOCOLS

2.5.1 Shorts shall not be worn when the ambient temperature is below 10°C, unless paired with visible leg warmers, or protected by self-delusion.

– Riders who appear immune to cold shall not be cited, but shall be treated with respectful confusion.

– Clause 2.5.1a: Riders turning up in shorts and no gloves in winter will not be sanctioned, but may be nominated for group folklore status.

2.5.2 Spring and Autumn attire misjudgements are considered non-citable under the "Should've Brought the Gilet" Clause.

– However, sarcasm, teasing, and theatrical shivering or vice versa pretend overheating are encouraged and shall be protected speech.

.

§2.6 – New Rider Consideration Clause

2.6.1 Riders new to the discipline of group road cycling shall be granted clemency for kit-related crimes, including but not limited to:

- Mismatched socks,
- Mountain bike helmets,
- Bar ends,
- General "Decathlon Chic."

– These riders shall not receive formal citations, but will be gently nudged toward proper attire through cultural osmosis, passive comments, and increasingly unsubtle birthday gifts.

§2.7 – Enforcement and Discretion

2.7.1 Citations under Chapter 2 may be issued immediately by any rider with matching socks and a full zip jersey.

2.7.2 Appeals may be submitted only by riders whose clothing choices did *not* result in flapping, overheating, chafing, or social exclusion.

2.7.3 Repeat offences may escalate to **CCS 5: Banter Blackout**, particularly if combined with lateness (see §1.1.3) or half-wheeling (see future Chapter 4).

CHAPTER 3: THE WHATSAPP ACCORDS AND THE TREATY OF DIGITAL CONDUCT

In the beginning, the word was typed. And it was good. Then came the stickers, and the voice notes, and lo, the digital covenant descended into farce.

§3.1 – GROUP CHAT USAGE PROTOCOL

3.1.1 The official WhatsApp group shall be used primarily for the coordination of rides, the announcement of changes, and the sharing of vital logistical intelligence (weather alerts, route tweaks, café closures).
– Clause 3.1.1a: Use of the group to ask "What time?" for a ride already clearly stated in the chat history shall result in **CCS 1: THE GLANCE**, possibly followed by a screenshot of your own laziness.

3.1.2 Weekend ride posts must follow the Standardised Ride Declaration Format (SRDF):

"[Day], [Time], [Route Length], [Pace Type], [Start Location]"
– Example: "Sunday, 8am, 85km, steady/social, meet at war memorial."
– Deviations may result in sarcastic requests for clarification or a passive scheduling coup by another member.

3.1.3 Riders confirming attendance shall respond with a simple, text-based "In" or equivalent.
– Reactions, memes, or cryptic GIFs are not legally binding confirmations.

§3.2 – THE DIGITAL DECENCY DOCTRINE

3.2.1 Excessive non-ride-related chat (memes, personal health updates, unsolicited photos of dogs or children) must be quarantined within accepted social tolerance (three posts per weekday, one GIF

per weekend).
– Breach of these thresholds triggers **CCS 2: GROUP REMINDER**, typically issued as "Maybe time for a separate group?"

3.2.2 Voice notes longer than 20 seconds shall be considered acts of conversational aggression.
– Offenders shall be referred to **CLAUSE 3.2.2A: THE MUTING PROTOCOL**, under which group members may pre-emptively silence said rider for 7 days.

3.2.3 The unsolicited sharing of one's own ride data, such as "just a quick 60km before breakfast," must be accompanied by self-deprecation or disclaimers of guilt.
– Arrogant uploads shall be punished by **CCS 3: CAFÉ TAX**, payable in smugness offsets.

§3.3 – THE RIDE CANCELLATION CLAUSE

3.3.1 No ride shall be cancelled due to weather unless:
(a) The Met Office has issued a named storm,
(b) Visibility is sub-fog, or
(c) Ice has formed on the inside of your windows.

3.3.2 Cancellations must be announced at least 60 minutes prior to departure with photographic evidence and supporting data.
– Riders issuing false or cowardly cancellations shall be subject to **CCS 4: TRIBUNAL**, particularly if the sun emerges an hour later.

§3.4 – THE "STILL ON?" OFFENCE

3.4.1 Any rider who messages "Still on?" within 15 minutes of ride time (or, Heaven forbid, at the exact meeting time) shall be issued a formal citation.
– First offence: **CCS 2: GROUP REMINDER**
– Repeat offence: **CCS 5: BANTER BLACKOUT**, with all "In/Out" responses ignored for 14 days.
– Clause 3.4.1a: The "Just Checking" Defence is not admissible.

§3.5 – GROUP CHAT GOVERNANCE

3.5.1 Admin privileges shall be granted only to riders who meet three of the following five criteria:

- Own more than two bikes
- Know how to use Komoot without crashing the app
- Are not chronically late (see §1.1.3)
- Have never sent a 3-minute voice note
- Can spell "definitely" without autocorrect

3.5.2 Removal of a member from the chat (see CCS 6) must be agreed by at least two admins or one ride captain and the group's fastest hill climber.

§3.6 – LOCAL CUSTOMISATION CLAUSE

3.6.1 Groups may opt to use alternative platforms (Telegram, Signal, carrier pigeon), but such decisions must be ratified via meme-based vote.
3.6.2 Seasonal emoji themes (e.g. snowflakes for

winter rides, beer mugs post-ride) are permitted but must not exceed three in a single message unless for satirical purposes.

§3.7 – ENFORCEMENT AND SATIRE RIGHTS

3.7.1 All riders have the right to enforce these laws through sarcasm, overuse of the 😎 emoji, or strategic message liking.
3.7.2 All citations issued under Chapter 3 shall include a mandatory screenshot for evidence and eternal shame.

CHAPTER 4: THE GRAND CONVENTION OF PACK RIDING

And the riders rode two by two, unless they didn't, in which case chaos ensued.

§4.1 - THE LAW OF TWO ABREAST

4.1.1 The default riding formation shall be two abreast, evenly matched in power, tempo, and conversational ability.
— Deviating to three abreast is permitted only in controlled conditions, such as closed roads or during heated debates about tyre pressure.
— Riders failing to close the gap and drifting off the back mid-conversation shall be issued **CCS 1: THE GLANCE** and moved to conversational probation.

4.1.2 Single file shall only be adopted:
(a) On narrow roads where a tractor could maul the group,
(b) When being shouted at by a motorist with a visible vein in their temple,
(c) Under the *"Just for a bit"* Agreement, which shall not exceed 2km.

§4.2 - THE ANTI-HALF-WHEELING EDICT

4.2.1 Half-wheeling is defined as riding imperceptibly ahead of your companion while claiming to "just be tapping along."
— This is an act of psychological warfare and shall be punished without mercy.
— First offence: verbal warning.
— Second offence: **CCS 2: GROUP REMINDER** with full name mention.
— Third offence: **CCS 4: TRIBUNAL**, where a public dissection of character and wattage insecurity shall take place.

§4.3 – Rotation Rituals

4.3.1 All rotations shall proceed in a clockwise direction, unless otherwise dictated by the Ride Leader, local bylaws, or wind-induced crisis.
– *Clause 4.3.1a:* Should the group fail to execute a clean rotation three consecutive times, the strongest rider shall be condemned to sit on the front until morale improves or they admit they've been watching too many classics replays.

4.3.2 In standard double paceline operation, riders on the front shall peel off as a pair, drifting outward and rearward in a dignified fashion, without flinching, surging, or initiating philosophical discussion mid-manoeuvre.

4.3.3 In chain gang formations, the lead rider shall initiate transition using the Standardised Elbow Flick (SEF).
– The elbow flick shall be:
(a) Clear,
(b) Brief,
(c) Executed only to signal rotation,
(d) Never used for sarcasm, imitation, or greeting nearby livestock.

– Misuse of the elbow flick, especially in non-rotational contexts, shall result in **CCS 2: Group Reminder** and revocation of flicking privileges for one calendar week.

4.3.4 Riders dropping back shall do so smoothly, without:

- Sudden braking,

- Flailing gestures,

- Auditory declarations of doom ("I'M GONE!" is not protocol).

– The theatrical "my turn is done" wave is discouraged, unless collapsing dramatically is the only available means of saving face.

4.3.5 Riders surging into the wind during rotation, overtaking their own rotation partner, or generally making a scene shall receive **CCS 3: Café Tax**, payable to the nearest victim of their chaos.

§4.4 – WHEEL CONDUCT AND PROXIMITY LAW

4.4.1 A distance of 6-12 inches shall be maintained between front and rear wheels in pacelines.
– Excessive gaps create concertinas and the illusion of disinterest.
– Riding too close and overlapping wheels is reserved only for those with track experience or a death wish.

4.4.2 Touching wheels shall not be excused with the phrase "It's all part of the sport."
– It is not. It is how clavicles are broken. Repeat offenders shall be marked and exiled to the rear for a period of reflection.

§4.5 – GESTURES AND COMMUNICATION STANDARDS

4.5.1 All potholes, gravel, roadkill, and random craters shall be pointed out clearly, using the

internationally recognised point-and-shout method.
— Shouting "HOLE!" in a panicked falsetto is permitted and in some cases mandatory.
— Clause 4.5.1a: Failure to call out obstacles shall trigger **CCS 2**. If someone flatted due to your silence, escalation to **CCS 4** is automatic.

4.5.2 Signal communication must be clear, unified, and not resemble interpretive dance.
— Riders who wave cars through without checking shall be prosecuted under the *Implied Liability Act*, clause 2002b: "You waved, they hit us, it's your fault."

See Chapter 8 for detailed breakdown of signs and signals

§4.6 – THE REGROUP PACT

4.6.1 All climbs, headwind stretches, and natural selection zones must be followed by a regroup point, ideally in a layby, junction, or outside a bakery.
— Those who summit early must wait, offer snacks, and pretend not to be smug.

4.6.2 Riders failing to wait shall be branded with a **CCS 3**, and possibly reassigned to pull duty for the next 30km.

See Chapter 9 for further details

§4.7 – RIDE CAPTAIN AUTHORITY

4.7.1 The Ride Captain is granted full authority to call formations, halt the ride, or issue sarcastic commentary at will.

– Disputing a call mid-ride results in **CCS 5: BANTER BLACKOUT**, enforceable immediately and irrevocably.

§4.8 – LOCAL AMENDMENTS

4.8.1 In areas of high tourism, sheep traffic, or known angry postmen, formations may be altered by local statute.
4.8.2 Group may establish its own "agreed signals" but must post diagrams to the chat before enforcement.

CHAPTER 5: WEATHER PREPAREDNESS AND HONOUR IN THE FACE OF PRECIPITATION

And yea, the clouds did gather, and some turned back. And others pressed on, damp but righteous.

§5.1 - THE COVENANT OF CONTINUATION

5.1.1 The ride shall proceed unless conditions constitute a genuine threat to life, limb, or drivetrain. Acceptable causes for ride cancellation include:
(a) Ice,
(b) Surface flooding,
(c) Winds exceeding 40 km/h,
(d) Lightning near enough to smell it.
– Clause 5.1.1a: Drizzle is not dangerous. Riders refusing to ride in light rain shall be encouraged to explore the Zwift Redemption Path and post screenshots by way of atonement.

5.1.2 Any rider cancelling due to "CBA" must declare it openly. They shall be granted one "Cannot Be Arsed" token per quarter, with grace and understanding.
– Repeated CBA declarations shall result in **CCS 2: GROUP REMINDER**, phrased as "Mate, you've been CBA since September."

5.1.3 Riders attempting to blame the weather retroactively, when in fact they just didn't fancy it, shall be issued **CCS 1: THE GLANCE**, often followed by a forecast screenshot from someone who *did* ride.

§5.2 - ROUTE ADAPTATION IN THE FACE OF WIND AND WRATH

5.2.1 Where wind exceeds 20 km/h at ride start, route planning shall follow the Out-and-Back Headwind Doctrine:

"Out into the wind. Back with the smugness."
– Clause 5.2.1a: Wind below 20 km/h is classified as "bracing" and shall not influence route decisions, except for very light riders, defined as <60kg for males, <50kg for females.

§5.2.2: Sidewind-heavy routes shall be firmly avoided when forecasts predict gusts exceeding 30 km/h, as such conditions render pacelines chaotic, wheel overlap lethal, and group cohesion imaginary.
– Exceptions apply only to riders equipped with deep-section wheels (≥50mm) and a visible intent to suffer for the 'Gram.

– Clause 5.2.2a: Riders who knowingly brave sidewinds with deep rims, flappy jerseys, and a GoPro on the bars, solely to capture footage of themselves being violently side-shunted into a verge, shall be recognised under the Instagram Content Seeker's Exemption.
This exemption permits their participation, but also allows all other riders to:
(a) Decline to assist,
(b) Film their downfall,
(c) Issue **CCS 3: Café Tax** for any delay caused by their vanity.

– Clause 5.2.2b: Any rider whose Instagram post includes hashtags such as #crosswindwarrior, #rideordie, or #sailinoncarbon, shall forfeit the right to complain about stability, safety, or rim depth thereafter.

5.2.3 Riders insisting on "doing the hills" during storms shall be politely reassigned to solo suffering or Zwift penance.

§5.3 – ATTIRE EXPECTATIONS DURING WEATHER EVENTS

5.3.1 Riders attending during precipitation shall wear:

- Mudguards (long and functional),
- Waterproof gilet or jacket (bonus points if it doesn't flap),
- Overshoes (not plastic bags),
- Gloves (that are *gloves*, not thin regrets).

– Clause 5.3.1a: Riders without mudguards shall ride at the back, under the Wheel Spray Isolation Protocol.
– Clause 5.3.1b: Those who arrive in shorts under 5°C shall not be punished but instead quietly admired and slightly feared.

5.3.2 Thermal misjudgement in spring and autumn (e.g. boiling in a rain jacket, freezing in mesh base layer) shall not incur citation, but shall be met with sarcasm, sympathy, and retrospective weather chat for the remainder of the ride.

§5.4 – THE HONOUR OF THE HYPOTHERMIC BRAG

5.4.1 Post-ride commentary involving:

- Frozen fingers,
- Loss of feeling below the waist,
- Rain inside one's bib shorts,
  – shall be recognised as legitimate prestige

markers, provided they are delivered in a tone of stoic understatement, not attention-seeking martyrdom.

– Clause 5.4.1a: Use of the phrase "proper ride" in summary is permitted, encouraged, and in some groups, compulsory.

§5.5 – Weather Call Governance

5.5.1 The decision to cancel or amend a ride due to weather must be made no later than T0–20 minutes, unless ice forms after that in a cruel twist of fate.
– Group consensus is preferred. Failing that, the call falls to:
(a) The nominated ride leader,
(b) The rider with the most Rapha, or
(c) The oldest member present.

5.5.2 Riders who ignore the cancellation and go solo shall receive respectful mentions, but must post their ride on Strava within 30 minutes of returning, or it never happened.

§5.6 – Local Custom Clause

5.6.1 Regions with persistent drizzle, mild misery, or Scottish winter may revise the default thresholds.
– Clause 5.6.1a: In these locations, "wet" becomes a default state, and rides may only be cancelled by acts of God or road closure by local council.

CHAPTER 6: THE CAFÉ TAXATION PROTOCOLS AND RULES OF PASTRY ENGAGEMENT

And they did arrive at the café, wind-battered and sugar-depleted. And lo, one among them sprinted for the door. And he was cast out.

§6.1 - ARRIVAL ETIQUETTE AND SPRINT PROHIBITION

6.1.1 The approach to the café is a neutral zone. There shall be no sprinting, attacking, or surging once the café is within visible range. This zone begins at 1km to pastry, or at the first mention of "flat white."
– Violations result in CCS 3: Café Tax, payable in full to those still breathing hard at the table.

6.1.2 Riders shall dismount in an orderly fashion, refrain from cluttering entrances, and queue like functioning adults.
– Clause 6.1.2a: Riders who proceed straight to a table without ordering shall be referred to CCS 2, with a side of contempt.

§6.2 - TABLE PROTOCOL AND SEAT ASSIGNMENT

6.2.1 Tables shall not be claimed until the majority of the group has reached the café and is ready to sit.
– "I'm just holding it" is not a legal defence unless the rider is visibly shaking with hunger.

6.2.2 Outdoor seating shall be preferred unless;
(a) Hypothermia is imminent,
(b) Rain is horizontal,
(c) All gloves have already been removed.
– Indoors seating must be respectful, quiet, and mudguard-compatible. Woe unto those who leave tyre tracks on café furniture.

§6.3 - The Coffee & Cake Order of Precedence

6.3.1 Each rider shall queue and pay individually, or through a pre-agreed rotational system.

– Riders attempting the "Oh, can you grab me one?" move without financial follow-up shall be subject to CCS 4: Tribunal and a deep audit of past generosity.

6.3.2 Orders must not exceed two items per rider unless:
(a) Calories are visibly needed, or
(b) The rider is paying for another as penance (see §6.6.2).

6.3.3 The final pastry shall not be taken without first issuing a group-wide public offer.
– Clause 6.3.3a: If two riders claim it simultaneously, it shall be awarded to the most fatigued, as verified by visible facial collapse or audible stomach growling.

§6.4 – Food Conduct and Public Decency

6.4.1 Riders shall eat with dignity. No audible slurping, gel packets on plates, or visible chewing of protein bars still in foil.
– Clause 6.4.1a: Those who remove shoes indoors shall be issued CCS 5: Banter Blackout, effective immediately.

6.4.2 Non-cyclists must be treated with courtesy. This includes not staring at their sandwiches, explaining wattage unprompted, or loudly dissecting sprint finishes.
– The café is a place of rest and recovery, not data evangelism.

§6.5 – Phone Conduct and Strava Rituals

6.5.1 Phones shall remain off the table unless:
(a) Photographing cake for the group,
(b) Posting to Strava immediately post-coffee,
(c) Proving you really did ride here.

6.5.2 Strava uploads shall occur post-consumption, not during chewing, unless it's raining and the group wants to brag.

6.5.3 Rides posted to Strava tagging "Coffee stop included" must include the following emoji ☕ and picture of coffee art or coffee cup on a table with blurred background to ensure historical accuracy.

§6.6 – Punitive Purchases and Café Justice

6.6.1 Any rider who:

- Drops the group unnecessarily,

- Causes a mechanical through neglect,

- Arrives late without notifying the group,
  – shall cover the coffee and/or cake of at least two riders.

6.6.2 The Full Round Penalty is triggered for:
(a) Sprinting to the café,
(b) Wearing full aero kit for a recovery ride,
(c) Turning up with a gravel bike and pretending it's fine.
– Penalty is payable immediately. No IOUs. Cash or card. No cryptocurrency.

§6.7 – Exit Procedure and Re-Mounting Order

6.7.1 Riders shall not be the first to finish eating and the first to say "Right, let's roll." This is considered a violation of recovery norms.

6.7.2 Reapplication of gloves, helmets, and dignity shall occur in silence, punctuated only by espresso regret and saddle groaning.

6.7.3 Departures shall resume in standard formation, with no attacks until at least 3km post-cake digestion.

CHAPTER 7: FUELLING, FEEDING, AND THE GEL WRAPPER ACCOUNTABILITY ACT

And lo, in the second hour, energy did fade, spirits did falter, and the wise reached into their pockets and retrieved sustenance. But the foolish had brought nothing, and they were dropped like Pharaoh's army at the Red Sea.

§7.1 – Nutritional Self-Sufficiency Statute

7.1.1 All riders are solely responsible for their own caloric maintenance during the ride.
– Clause 7.1.1a: Asking for food is permitted only under emergency bonk conditions, defined as:
(a) Loss of speech,
(b) Loss of coasting ability,
(c) Eyes going to sleep.
– Offenders may be granted a bar but shall receive CCS 2: Group Reminder, and are required to over-compensate on the next ride.

7.1.2 Fuelling shall be planned based on ride duration and intensity:

<1.5 hours: optional light snack.

1.5-3 hours: one solid item and one gel or equivalent.

3 hours: full buffet in pockets, ideally colour-coded and waterproofed.
– Clause 7.1.2a: Riders with nothing but water and vibes after 60 minutes shall be known as The Fasting Brigade, and will be gently shamed in a well-meaning, public manner.

§7.2 – Timing of Intake Clause

7.2.1 Food shall be consumed:

- Every 40-60 minutes on longer rides,
- At the top of hills (not during),
- With silent chewing and minimal packet noise.

- Slick hand action into and out of pockets and requisite return of over garments to cover pockets, preventing the disgrace of a wonky garment.

7.2.2 Eating on the bike must not:
(a) Interfere with safe handling,
(b) Cause wrappers to drift into the path of others,
(c) Be accompanied by the phrase "I just need a quick snack," which is universally understood as "drop me."

§7.3 – ACCEPTABLE EDIBLES FRAMEWORK

- 7.3.1 Approved on-ride nutrition includes:

- Energy bars,

- Gels (used responsibly),

- Bananas (ideally intact),

- Cake wrapped in foil (old school, high prestige),

- Homemade snacks (immediate status boost).

– Clause 7.3.1a: Non-foods (protein bars, jerky, soup) are subject to CCS 1: The Glance unless explained in detail and with sincere regret.

7.3.2 Gels must be consumed in silence. Do not narrate it.
– Any comment resembling "this is a game-changer" or "new flavour just dropped" shall result in CCS 2, with potential escalation.

§7.4 – Littering and Wrapper Management Act

7.4.1 All packaging shall be retained on one's person. Pockets are the designated bin.
– Clause 7.4.1a: Riders who eject gel wrappers onto the Queen's highway shall be subject to immediate CCS 6: Ejection and possible real-world legal intervention.

7.4.2 Mid-ride unwrapping shall be performed with minimal rustle, maximum grace, and no impact on group cohesion.
– The "One-Handed Banana Skin Flick" is a recognised Level 5 skill.
– Dropping a bar, then stopping the group to retrieve it, is punishable with a Café Tax under §6.6.1.

§7.5 – Emergency Feeding Clause

7.5.1 In the event of a full bonk, the following procedure shall occur:
(a) Rider confesses with dignity ("I've got nothing left"),
(b) Nearest rider administers food and sympathy,
(c) Group reduces pace for no less than 7 minutes,
(d) Café stop is upgraded to include warm beverage and cake with icing.

7.5.2 The bonked rider shall repay all donations within 14 days, either in goods or favourable pulls into headwinds.

§7.6 - Non-Sanctioned Fuel Sources

7.6.1 Consumption of any of the following during rides is discouraged:

- Boiled eggs,
- Loose trail mix,
- Unwrapped flapjacks disintegrating in pockets,
- Salty snacks not offered to others,
- Roadkill.

7.6.2 Any rider producing crinkly, elaborate, or excessive picnic setups shall be issued CCS 3: Café Tax, payable in aesthetic damage control.

§7.7 – The Glucose Recovery Blessing

7.7.1 Riders may give thanks at ride's end for the simple blessings of sugar, caffeine, and the mate who always brings "a spare gel, just in case."
– This is a non-binding, spiritually encouraged clause.

CHAPTER 8: SAFETY, SIGNALS, AND THE SACRED ACT OF SHOUTING "CAR BACK!"

And lo, the peloton did ride in harmony, and they did point, and they did call, and all were safe. Until Dave swerved into a pothole while eating a fig bar and chaos descended once more.

§8.1 – The Sacred Signals Codex

8.1.1 All riders shall issue hand signals clearly, early, and without interpretive flair, unless expressly trained in semaphore.
– Acceptable gestures include:
(a) Turns: full arm or stiff-fingered point,
(b) Stopping/slowing: flat palm down,
(c) Potholes: sharp downward point,
(d) Debris: jazz hands permitted only here,
(e) Obstruction/pedestrian: behind-the-back sweep or an exasperated shrug.

8.1.2 Signal failure resulting in braking, swerving or near-collision shall trigger **CCS 4: Tribunal**, with required hand demonstration at the next café stop, using condiments for visual aid.

§8.2 – Verbal Communication Statute

8.2.1 Riders shall speak with sufficient volume and clarity, even if it risks revealing their true FTP.
– Standard calls include:
"Car back!",
"Hole!",
"Stopping!",
"Rider down!",
"Dog!", and
in rare instances, "Deer!"

8.2.2 All vocal calls must be passed up/down the line. Riders who receive and suppress critical information shall be identified as Communication Bottlenecks and issued CCS 2 and forced to lead the next rotation into a headwind.

§8.2.3 - Prohibition of "CLEAR!" at Junctions
The call "CLEAR!" is strictly prohibited at all junctions, roundabouts, and crossings unless the rider issuing it is:
(a) Legally authorised,
(b) Wearing a fluorescent sash, and
(c) Employed to control traffic.

– Shouting "CLEAR!" transfers liability, creates false confidence, and encourages following riders to proceed without checking for themselves.
– Riders must assess the road independently, using their own eyes and judgement, not someone else's optimism.

Violations will trigger:

- **CCS 5: Banter Blackout**, and

- A mandatory public reading of the Highway Code, with particular emphasis on Rule 170.

Riders may instead use appropriate calls such as:

- "Car left,"

- "Car right,"

- "Slowing,"

- "Stopping,"
  – All of which describe, not instruct.

§8.3 – LINE DISCIPLINE AND PREDICTABILITY PROVISION

8.3.1 All riders must hold a consistent line unless avoiding:
(a) Death,
(b) Debris, or
(c) Children on scooters.

8.3.2 Lateral drift, wheel overlap, and last-minute braking are to be avoided unless one desires immediate demotion to the rear and a group therapy session at the next stop.

8.3.3 Out-of-saddle surges shall be preceded by a subtle rise from the saddle and a promise not to rocket backwards like a startled mule.

§8.4 – DESCENT LAW AND THE GRAVITY ACCORD

8.4.1 Descending shall be approached with grace, modesty, and brakes that work.
– Excessive aero tucks are permitted only for certified nutcases or YouTubers wearing GoPros.

8.4.2 Riders overtaking on descents must ensure:
(a) Space,
(b) No squeaky brakes, and
(c) That the manoeuvre isn't just to prove something to themselves.

8.4.3 Braking hard mid-descent without warning is an act of mechanical treason. The group reserves the right to relegate such offenders to **CCS 3: CAFÉ TAX** and permanent rear-guard duty.

§8.5 - THE "CAR BACK" CANON

8.5.1 "Car back!" shall be announced with moderate urgency and passed up the peloton like the sacred call it is.
– The correct volume is "firm but not terrified."

8.5.2 Upon hearing "Car back!", the group shall SINGLE OUT SMOOTHLY, not scatter like startled pigeons.
– Riders who do not respond to the call due to pride, deafness, or ego shall be documented for **CCS 2: GROUP REMINDER**.

8.5.3 "Car Up?" is to be used for referring to vehicles infront and not behind for it is decreed that car up does not refer to a vehicle behind. Explanations that "The car is UP your bum!", is subject to deep disdain.

§8.6 - MECHANICAL MERCY AND GROUP CONSCIENCE

8.6.1 Any mechanical failure–flat, dropped chain, or electronic despair–must be clearly declared.
– Silence is not stoicism. It's sabotage.

8.6.2 The group shall stop unless in a race simulation (declared at ride start) or unless the afflicted is Dave and this is the fourth flat in two weeks.

8.6.3 Riders receiving mechanical assistance must say "Thank you." Multiple times. In sincere tones.

§8.7 - THE UNIVERSAL SALUTE CLAUSE

8.7.1 All cyclists must acknowledge all other cyclists, without exception, unless navigating a roundabout, a

near-death moment, or sipping coffee mid-ride.
– Approved gestures:
(a) The hand wave (preferred),
(b) The nod (acceptable),
(c) The eyebrow lift (borderline),
(d) The full palm (classic),
(e) Verbal greeting ("Morning!", "Alright?") when energy permits.

8.7.2 Children on bikes, pensioners on trikes, and adults on shopping baskets shall be acknowledged with a mild nod and a respectful smile.
– Clause 8.7.2a: Electric cargo bikes piloted by flustered parents are to be met with reverence.

8.7.3 Triathletes are permitted to acknowledge runners, as a gesture of solidarity in lonely suffering.

8.7.4 Failure to acknowledge fellow riders is punishable by **CCS 1: THE GLANCE**, which may evolve into **CCS 2** if repeated within a 10km stretch.

§8.8 – HAPPENCHANCE LINK-UP AND WHEEL-SITTING ETIQUETTE

8.8.1 When a stranger joins the group mid-ride, basic etiquette dictates:
(a) A nod or smile,
(b) A greeting,
(c) Permission before sitting on a wheel for longer than 60 seconds.

8.8.2 Sitting silently on the wheel of a stranger without warning shall trigger immediate suspicion, side-eyes, and a **SLOW-DOWN TEST**.

– If they pass the test (i.e. acknowledge and hold their line), they may remain.

– If not, they shall be dropped at the next incline with quiet cruelty.

8.8.3 If *you* are the stranger, you must:

- Announce your presence,

- Ask to join, and

- Offer at least one anecdote or compliment about the weather, kit, or café quality.

– Breach of this results in **CCS 3** and being sent to the front with zero context.

CHAPTER 8A: THE COVENANT OF COURTESY – PASSING HORSES, SHEEP, AND PEDESTRIANS WITHOUT INCIDENT OR INFAMY

And lo, there were creatures of hoof and foot upon the road, and they did not hear thy freehub, nor fear thy Lycra. And thus the wise did pass with reverence, and the foolish did spook the mare and were cast into the hedge.

§8A.1 – THE EQUINE ENGAGEMENT PROTOCOL

8a.1.1 When approaching horses, the peloton shall reduce speed to below 15 km/h and switch to single file no less than 25 metres before contact range.
– Riders shall announce themselves clearly and calmly, using words not shrieks.
– Approved phrase: "Morning! Passing on your right!"
– Forbidden phrase: "Whoa!" unless one is a cowboy.

8a.1.2 Riders must avoid:
(a) Sudden braking,
(b) Loud freewheeling buzz,
(c) Wild gesticulation,
(d) Aero tucks within spooking distance.
– Violation triggers CCS 4: Tribunal, likely involving the horse's owner and several angry Facebook posts.

8a.1.3 All horses passed without incident shall be met with a nod to the rider and verbal thanks, even if the horse did nothing but judge you silently.

§8A.2 – LIVESTOCK RESPECT DIRECTIVE

8a.2.1 When encountering loose sheep, cows, or goats, riders shall:

- Slow to walking pace,

- Avoid noises (bells or voices),

- Not attempt to herd unless qualified in agricultural matters.

8a.2.2 If livestock are crossing, the group shall halt and observe with silent reverence.
– Those who attempt to ride through a flock shall be subject to CCS 6: Group Ejection, and possibly added to the farmer's eternal blacklist.

8a.2.3 Riders who photograph animals must do so quietly and respectfully, avoiding selfies, loud commentary, or impersonations.

§8A.3 – PEDESTRIAN PASSING CODE

8a.3.1 When passing pedestrians, especially on shared paths, riders shall:

Slow down,

Verbally warn of approach ("Coming by on your right!"),

Leave at least 1 metre where possible.
– Clause 8a.3.1a: Use of bells is encouraged where available, so long as it is chimed, not rung like a fire alarm.

8a.3.2 Passing families, dog walkers, or Nordic walkers shall be done with patience and respect.
– Passive sighing or tutting triggers **CCS 2: GROUP REMINDER** and reassignment to polite training rides.

8a.3.3 Dogs shall be treated as SENTIENT, unpredictable hazards with high random movement potential.
– Riders shall prepare for sudden lunges, extend maximum clearance, and never, under any

circumstance, utter "He's fine" unless the dog is actually theirs.

§8A.4 – ENCOUNTER SUMMARY AND COURTESY MANDATE

8a.4.1 Upon successfully navigating any human or animal obstacle, riders shall offer a verbal thank you, nod, Alan Shearer one-hand signal, or two-finger salute (friendly version).
– Clause 8a.4.1a: If no acknowledgement is returned, riders must not mutter, "Well, that's rude." You are not the main character.

8a.4.2 Any rider who causes a horse to spook, a pedestrian to leap, or a sheep to bolt shall receive **CCS 5: BANTER BLACKOUT**, and be known, henceforth, as *The Startler*.

CHAPTER 9: CLIMBING, DROPPING, AND THE BROTHERHOOD OF THE REGROUP

*And lo, the gradient increased, and so did the self-delusion.
And some did dance, and some did grind, and some did
wheeze like a punctured bellows—but all were judged.*

§9.1 – The Climb Declaration Protocol

9.1.1 All significant climbs (classified as: >500m in length or >4% gradient) shall be announced ahead of time, either verbally or via route briefing.
– Clause 9.1.1a: The phrase *"it kicks up a bit"* is acceptable, but must not be used to describe 12% ramps. This is linguistic fraud and punishable by **CCS 2: Group Reminder**.

9.1.2 Climbs shall be approached in a spirit of personal challenge, mutual tolerance, and silent suffering.
– Riders who attempt conversation mid-climb must either be quieted or conscripted into coaching duties.

§9.2 – Effort Honour Code

9.2.1 All riders are free to climb at their own pace. Those who wish to ascend with style, panache, and ill-advised enthusiasm shall be permitted to do so–but must wait at the top.
– Clause 9.2.1a: "Just tapping out a tempo" while visibly sprinting past others shall be considered *passive-aggressive climbing* and merits **CCS 1: The Glance**.

9.2.2 No rider shall feign surprise at their own climbing form if they:
(a) Rode every hill like it was an escape attempt,
(b) Train six days a week, or
(c) Consistently pass others while saying "I'm feeling slow today."

– Violators shall receive **CCS 4: TRIBUNAL**, where wine intake and cheese-based snacking will be reviewed in detail.

9.2.3 Moaning about climbing performance while consuming excess dairy, alcohol, or sedentary television drama shall be recorded under Clause 9.2.3a: Lifestyle Incompatibility Syndrome (LIS).
– Treatment includes honesty, hydration, and fewer brie-based dinners.

§9.3 – THE DROP AWARENESS ACT

9.3.1 Riders who drop others mid-climb shall, at the summit, initiate the Regroup Protocol:
(a) Cease pedalling,
(b) Offer breathless nods to approaching riders,
(c) Avoid phrases like "I thought you were right there!" unless followed by snacks.

9.3.2 Riders who deliberately attack just before the summit to cause a gap shall be issued **CCS 3: CAFÉ TAX**, payable to the first victim to roll over the crest, gasping.

9.3.3 Riders who were dropped but rejoin shall not be subjected to interrogation, pity, or offers of gels unless specifically requested.

§9.4 – THE REGROUP MANDATE

9.4.1 All riders shall wait at a logical, safe location post-climb:

- Laybys,

- Summits with visibility,

- Cafés with cake.

– Waiting at the brow of a 14% blind corner is expressly forbidden.

9.4.2 Regrouping must include at least 90 seconds of stop time, during which riders may:
(a) Breathe,
(b) Adjust garments,
(c) Reassess life choices.
– Clause 9.4.2a: "Let's roll" before the last rider arrives is a **CCS 2** offence and an abuse of tempo control.

§9.5 – CLIMBING COMMENTARY RESTRICTIONS

9.5.1 Phrases prohibited during climbing include:

"Is this the top?"

"I'm not built for this,"

"It's steeper than it looks,"

"I'm at 300w here"

"I've not been riding much," (especially if false).

9.5.2 Approved commentary, if required, includes:

"Dig in,"

"All the way to the tree,"

"It levels out… eventually."

9.5.3 Praise of another's climbing must not be sarcastic, unless visibly justified by gear choice, cadence, or pained facial expression.

§9.6 - KOM Ethics and Honourable Theft Clause

9.6.1 Should a rider accidentally claim a STRAVA KOM/QOM, they must confess if:
(a) They were wheel-sucking,
(b) They had a tailwind,
(c) They were doing an FTP test and forgot the hill was there.

9.6.2 Riders planning a KOM attempt must announce intentions at the base and not use "Oh I was just feeling good" as post hoc justification.
– Failure to announce shall result in **CCS 5: Banter Blackout**, especially if gloating is involved.

CHAPTER 10: THE DESCENT PACT AND THE COVENANT OF CORNERING

And the road did turn downward, and some rejoiced, and some braked, and some clenched like frightened mortals. And in the corners, truth was revealed—and sometimes, wheels were lost.

§10.1 - THE DESCENT PACT

10.1.1 Upon commencement of a descent, all riders shall enter into the sacred **DESCENT PACT**, agreeing to:
(a) Ride within personal limits,
(b) Maintain adequate spacing, and
(c) Not die.

10.1.2 Riders who descend like lunatics shall announce their intention with "Coming by on your right," not with a sudden whir of carbon and a plume of existential dread.

10.1.3 Riders who are less confident shall remain:
(a) On the inside line wherever possible,
(b) Predictable,
(c) Aware that braking is not a character flaw.
– Clause 10.1.3a: Any rider shamed for descending cautiously shall trigger **CCS 3: CAFÉ TAX**, paid to the victim, who is probably still descending.

10.1.4 There shall be no overtaking unless there is ample space, zero surprise, and full certainty that the other rider isn't going to have a wobble and ruin everything.

10.1.5 If one crashes on a descent, all commentary must begin with "Glad you're okay" before any mocking of cornering technique may commence.

§10.2 - THE CORNERING CODE OF CONDUCT

10.2.1 All corners shall be approached with humility, not hubris. Riders must not:

- Divebomb corners,
- Cut inside on group rides,
- Apex like a MotoGP wildcard.

10.2.2 Riders shall call out "Slowing" or "Sharp corner" in advance if visibility or grip conditions warrant it.
– Clause 10.2.2a: Calling "Gravel!" shall be treated as gospel. The group will accept this call with instant reverence, regardless of severity.

10.2.3 Riders shall give plenty of room, particularly if:

- It has rained in the last 12 hours,
- There are wet leaves, diesel rainbows, or horse byproducts,
- The road surface looks like God gave up laying it halfway through.

10.2.4 Riders who enjoy cornering shall be considered slightly unwell, but tolerated provided they pass others cleanly, without sneering or doing that lean-over-the-bars thing they saw on GCN.
– Clause 10.2.4a: Verbal analysis of lines and apexes post-corner is limited to 10 seconds and must be requested, not volunteered.

10.2.5 Riders who deliberately steer clear of fast cornering are not to be mocked but respected. They have seen things.

§10.3 – Descent Communication and Etiquette

10.3.1 Calls during descents shall be:

- Clear ("Slowing!"),
- Calm ("Hole middle!"),
- Minimal ("Left!").

– Yelling "WHEEEEEE!" is permitted only under the Joyful Descent Clause, and only if not near livestock, joggers, or traffic.

10.3.2 All braking must be done early and gently, not mid-corner like someone realising they've made a terrible mistake.

10.3.3 Dropping your bottle, your chain, or your soul mid-descent does not exempt you from regrouping at the bottom. No excuses. Everyone waits. Unless they don't like you.

§10.4 – Descent Respect and the Cold Truth of Gravity

10.4.1 Riders who descend significantly faster than others shall:
(a) Wait at the bottom,
(b) Not gloat,
(c) Offer route intel like "Watch the second corner," not "That was easy."
– Clause 10.4.1a: Pointing out someone's braking point is a **CCS 2** unless you're related by blood or married.

10.4.2 Riders shall not compare descending speeds on Strava segments unless the descent is straight, dry, and has barriers, paramedics, and a waiver.

10.4.3 No rider shall utter "It's not that bad" on a descent until they have personally escorted another rider through it, at their pace, with a cheery disposition and a brake check.

CHAPTER 11: MECHANICAL MISCONDUCT AND THE CURSE OF THE UNMAINTAINED DRIVETRAIN

*And a sound did come forth from the rear derailleur—
clicketh, crunch, and squeal. And lo, the chain was dry, the
tubeless did leak, and all faith in their mechanical
stewardship was lost.*

§11.1 – Drivetrain Diligence Decree

11.1.1 All riders shall present themselves and their machines in fit mechanical order, defined by:

Clean, lubricated chain,

Quiet drivetrain,

Brakes that stop rather than whimper.

11.1.2 A squeaky chain shall be treated as an offence against the peace, the group, and the ancient gods of Campagnolo.
— First offence: **CCS 1: The Glance**
— Second: **CCS 4: Tribunal**, including a public recitation of "How to Apply Lube."

11.1.3 Riders whose chains look like they were stored in a canal must not offer excuses about "saving weight" by skipping maintenance.
— Clause 11.1.3a: If chain grime is audible, visible, or capable of leaving a mark on someone else's sock, the rider shall ride at the back, in shame.

§11.2 – The Puncture and Tubeless Horror Clause

11.2.1 All riders shall carry puncture provisions appropriate to their setup, including but not limited to:

Tube (or two),

Tubeless plug kit,

Pump or CO_2,

Stoicism.

11.2.2 Tubeless tyre failures are a special category of disgrace.
– Clause 11.2.2a: Riders who spray white latex across the bunch shall be met with groans, laughter, and disgrace, and will be known temporarily as The Leaker or Milky Spurter.
– Juvenile jokes are not only permitted–they are expected.

11.2.3 Should a rider take longer than 8 minutes to repair a puncture, the group may begin timing, commentating, and offering unsolicited advice.
– "Still at it?" is permitted at the 10-minute mark.
– "Would you like me to call someone?" is compulsory at 15.

§11.3 – THE TUBE RESPONSIBILITY ACT

11.3.1 Riders who request a spare tube must:
(a) Display genuine mechanical distress,
(b) Express gratitude,
(c) Repay the debt within 7 days or via **CCS 3: CAFÉ TAX**.
– Clause 11.3.1a: "I'll replace it next week" is the tube-borrower's version of "I'll call you."

11.3.2 Repeat borrowers shall be known as The Tube Lender's Burden, and must ride with a sticker reading "No spares, no shame."

§11.4 – Cleaning, Wiping, and Post-Repair Decency

11.4.1 Upon completing a mechanical repair, riders may clean hands only using:
(a) Grass,
(b) Moss,
(c) Their own kit.
– Clause 11.4.1a: Wet wipes are banned. We ride bikes, not babysit toddlers.

11.4.2 Riders who try to clean chain grease using a banana skin, a discarded tissue, or a gel wrapper shall receive **CCS 2**, and be placed under observation.

§11.5 – Accident Response and Hierarchy of Concern

11.5.1 In the event of a crash, riders shall assess injuries in order of priority:

- Consciousness,
- Bleeding,
- Bike.

11.5.2 Once a rider is confirmed alive, breathing, and mostly functional, it is permissible–in fact, expected–to ask:

"Is the bike okay?"
– Clause 11.5.2a: This question is not acceptable in hospitals or funerals. Allow a cooling off period of at least 3 weeks.

11.5.3 Riders involved in a crash may not deny assistance unless:
(a) They are clearly fine and overly dramatic,
(b) They refuse on principle,
(c) They are still tangled in the bike and can't actually speak.

§11.6 - MECHANICAL ATONEMENT PROTOCOL

11.6.1 Riders with chronic mechanical issues shall:

- Seek help,

- Watch tutorials,

- Admit they're bad at this and stop pretending otherwise.

11.6.2 Riders whose bikes emit noises resembling rodents, tectonic plates, or medieval torture shall be told bluntly:

"Your bike's not fine."
– There is no shame in ignorance. There is only shame in denial.

CHAPTER 12: THE LAVATORIAL CODEX – LAWFUL RELIEF AND MID-RIDE MICTURITION

And nature did call, as it always does—mid-ride and mid-nowhere. And the riders looked upon hedges, laybys, and the rear of unattended tractors. Some choices were noble. Others... less so. Thus is established the lawful doctrine of roadside urination.

§12.1 – THE RIGHT TO RELIEVE CLAUSE

12.1.1 All cyclists possess the inalienable right to relieve themselves mid-ride, without ridicule or shame, provided the act is executed with:
(a) Modesty
(b) Discretion
(c) Respect for flora, fauna, and the sanctity of local property

12.1.2 This right is immediately suspended if any of the following are true:

- The act is visible from an A-road or roundabout

- A school, playground, or licensed premises is within 100 metres

- The rider maintains eye contact with any pedestrian, jogger, or sheep during the act

§12.2 – DESIGNATED RELIEF ZONES

12.2.1 Lawful urination locations include:

- Hedgerows of sufficient density

- Behind parked, non-operational tractors

- Woodland edges or copse entrances

- Unoccupied agricultural buildings (e.g., barn doors ajar)

- The eighth tree after a summit (as per tradition)

12.2.2 UNACCEPTABLE SITES INCLUDE:

- Gateways
- Private driveways (no matter how rural)
- Café car parks
- Phone boxes (still illegal)
- The inside of one's own bib shorts (triathlon rules do not apply here)

12.2.3 Poor site selection shall trigger a **CCS 2: Group Reminder**, likely delivered via photo meme, and followed by mild social shunning at the next coffee stop.

§12.3 – PREVENTATIVE MEASURES AND PRE-RIDE PLANNING

12.3.1 All riders are expected to:

- Pee before departure
- Moderate caffeine intake to below the urinary threshold
- Avoid "hydration heroics" unless the ambient temperature exceeds 25°C

12.3.2 Failure to pre-emptively relieve oneself, then requesting a stop within the first 15km, shall be met with:

CCS 1: The Glance

Mandatory repositioning to the rear of the group until bladder stability is re-established

§12.4 – GROUP PEE STOP PROTOCOL

12.4.1 When one stops, many shall stop. This maintains both solidarity and plausible deniability. Riders shall form an inverse semi-circle, not a urinary conga line, and shall avoid all commentary during proceedings.

12.4.2 Riders who finish first must not roll ahead, as this triggers panic and performance anxiety in the still-streaming.

12.4.3 Riders identifying as female shall be afforded:
(a) Protective body coverage via the barrier formation
(b) Additional time, space, and absolute silence
(c) A minimum 60-second joke moratorium, enforceable by **CCS 5: Banter Blackout** if breached

§12.5 – EMERGENCY RELIEF PROCEDURES

12.5.1 In populated or town environments, riders requiring facilities must:
(a) Locate public toilets, petrol stations, or hospitable cafés
(b) Offer compensatory purchase if entering commercial premises
(c) Not ask, "Can I use your toilet?" in a tone implying that the answer is irrelevant

12.5.2 Riders suffering complete bladder failure mid-ride shall be granted the Amnesty of Immediate Forgetting.
It shall not be mentioned for the remainder of the season, except at the Christmas social in haiku form.

§12.6 – RE-ENTRY PROTOCOL POST-RELIEF

12.6.1 Riders must:

- Re-tuck

- Zip where has been unzipped

- Re-mount

- Re-integrate with the group silently and efficiently

12.6.2 Riders who fail to zip, adjust, or otherwise restore order to their lower garments shall receive **CCS 1**, and have all resulting photographic evidence held in digital escrow for future leverage.

§12.7 – DRIBBLE TOLERANCE AND ACCEPTABLE DAMPNESS PROTOCOL

12.7.1 Riders shall, upon completion of relief, take appropriate measures to ensure minimum visible wetting of shorts or legs. Acceptable residual dampness is defined as:

- No greater than a 5 cm radius dark patch

- No lower than mid-thigh in location

- No visible trickle lines below the hem of the bib short

12.7.2 Patches exceeding these limits shall be classified as a Category D Visual Leak, and subject to:

- CCS 1: The Glance

- Relocation to the downwind position in the bunch

- Optional towel-based mockery at the café

12.7.3 In warm weather (above 22°C), drying time shall be presumed rapid and forgiveness accelerated.
In cold weather (below 10°C), the group shall collectively pretend they didn't see it, unless photographic evidence is obtained.

12.7.4 Riders visibly proud of their overspill or who use it as a badge of riding authenticity shall be referred to the Disciplinary Board of Boundary Fluids for evaluation.

CHAPTER 13: NOVICES, INVITED GUESTS, AND THE SOCIAL CONTRACT OF INCLUSION

And the stranger did appear at the meeting point—helmet askew, bottle in the wrong cage, saddle too low—and the peloton looked upon them and said: "Welcome, but here are the rules."

§13.1 – THE OBLIGATION OF DISCLOSURE

13.1.1 Any rider inviting a guest or novice to the group shall be held personally responsible for explaining:

- The route,

- The pace,

- The café etiquette,

- The social rules,

- And the penalties for breaches (see Cyclist Citation System).

13.1.2 Failure to explain the basics before the ride begins—thereby exposing the guest to public shame, uncontrolled half-wheeling, or unsolicited aerodynamic advice—shall result in **CCS 3: CAFÉ TAX**, payable to the injured party *and* their chaperone.

13.1.3 The phrase "They'll be fine" is hereby banned unless:
(a) The guest is a current national champion,
(b) You've actually ridden with them before,
(c) You're willing to ride at their pace for the entire duration.

§13.2 – ONBOARDING ETIQUETTE AND THE AVOIDANCE OF HAZING

13.2.1 New riders shall be welcomed with a mix of:

- Warmth,

- Sarcasm,

- Low expectations.

13.2.2 Their kit shall not be judged unless it:
(a) Flaps,
(b) Is inside out,
(c) Includes arm warmers *and* a vest on a 28°C day.

– Clause 13.2.2a: All new riders are granted a three-ride grace period before fashion citations or drivetrain commentary may be issued.

13.2.3 Positioning within the group shall be arranged to protect the novice from:

Side winds,

Pace surges,

Conversations about cheese.

13.2.4 The act of "dropping the new one to teach them a lesson" is not tradition. It is a crime.
– First-time offenders receive **CCS 4: TRIBUNAL**, and must ride with a full frame pump for two weeks.

§13.3 – THE "NO-DROP" DOCTRINE AND ACCEPTABLE DEVIATIONS

13.3.1 Any ride advertised or declared as "no-drop" must adhere to the following guidelines:

- Regroup at all major summits,

- Slow or stop for mechanicals,

- Maintain verbal check-ins every 15–20 km.

13.3.2 Saying "No-drop" then slowly increasing the pace until only three remain is a known tactic referred

to as *the Hypocrite's Escalation* and is punishable by
CCS 5: BANTER BLACKOUT.

13.3.3 Exceptions to the "no-drop" rule may be
granted if:
(a) The dropped rider insists,
(b) GPS is available and functioning,
(c) The ride is being filmed for motivational content.

– Clause 13.3.3a: Riders invoking this exception must
post a follow-up message within 24 hours stating:
"They were fine and got back safely" accompanied by
proof-of-life Strava link.

§13.4 – GUEST ETIQUETTE

13.4.1 Invited guests shall:

- Introduce themselves,

- Ask questions,

- Sit in, observe, and *not surge off the front or
  immediately contest the first sprint.*

13.4.2 Guests who begin dishing out unsolicited
training advice, bar position critiques, or nutritional
strategies shall be told, politely but firmly to Foxtrot
Oscar, **CCS 6: The Ejection**.

13.4.3 Guests who impress without showing off,
contribute without dominating, and wait for the
group on hills shall be offered probationary banter
privileges and may receive early access to in-jokes.

§13.5 - INCLUSION CLAUSE

13.5.1 No rider shall be excluded for lack of speed, kit branding, or wheel choice—only for repeated violations of the Codex, dangerous behaviour, or being that guy.

13.5.2 The group shall be proactive in inviting those:

- New to the area,

- Returning from injury,

- Or attempting to shift from solo riding to social survival.

13.5.3 All group members must remember that they, too, were once a liability, and that somewhere out there, someone still remembers how they used to pedal like a startled foal.

CHAPTER 14: POST-RIDE DECORUM AND THE RITUAL OF THE STRAVA UPLOAD

And upon completion of the ride, it was decreed that one must not simply rest—but must publish. And the tribe gathered, and gave digital praise, and judged those who misrepresented metrics. For lo, the ride is not truly done until it has been documented, dissected, and admired— preferably before the first biscuit is eaten.

§14.1 – THE STATUTORY UPLOAD WINDOW

14.1.1 Upon cessation of cycling activity, riders shall initiate data upload proceedings within a reasonable temporal window, defined herein as:

T+30 minutes post-ride completion if signal permits,

T+2 hours if travel, café stops, or public relations interfere,

Before midnight under penalty of forgetfulness and omission.

14.1.2 Uploads delayed beyond this window without valid cause (e.g. device failure, crash, existential crisis) shall be considered in breach of the Completion Transparency Act, subject to a **CCS 2: GROUP REMINDER** and collective doubt.

§14.2 – RIDE TITLE LEGISLATION

14.2.1 Ride titles shall conform to the following acceptable formats:
(a) Factual descriptors (e.g. "Sunday Social," "North Loop"),
(b) Metric summaries (e.g. "100km of Why," "Hilly 80"),
(c) Humour permitted, but brevity enforced.

14.2.2 Titles must not include:

- Emotional backstory,
- Vague life lessons,
- Weather-based monologues,

- "Almost didn't go,"
- Or any mention of mindfulness unless the route passed a monastery.

14.2.3 Prohibited title infractions include:

- "Longest ride of the year!" (unless it objectively is),
- "Didn't feel great" (while averaging 35 km/h),
- "Just a spin" (if FTP was tested mid-ride).

– Infractions are punishable by **CCS 3: CAFÉ TAX**, payable to the most emotionally stable rider present.

§14.3 – SEGMENT ETHICS AND KOM/QOM DISCLOSURES

14.3.1 Any rider securing a crown or leaderboard position must disclose within the Strava description or comment if assisted by:
(a) Tailwind > 20 km/h,
(b) Group pacing,
(c) Motor vehicle adjacency,
(d) Aero enhancements of questionable taste.

14.3.2 Segment theft while drafting without permission, engaging in mid-ride deception, or deliberately hiding data constitutes an act of Leaderboard Malpractice and shall be investigated by the informal but feared Peloton Ethics Committee (PEC).

14.3.3 Riders achieving KOMs/QOMs while still under no-drop policy shall acknowledge domestiques by tag or tribute emoji.

§14.4 – KUDOS CODE OF OBLIGATION

14.4.1 Kudos shall be distributed in a timely and fair manner, with no regard for power output, equipment value, or sock length.
– Clause 14.4.1a: Failure to issue kudos for group rides one attended constitutes digital ingratitude and may result in **CCS 1: THE GLANCE**.

14.4.2 Riders found to kudo only elite performances, ignoring consistent or rehabilitative efforts, shall be subject to the Kudos Class Bias Review Panel (KCBRP).

14.4.3 Strategic withholding of kudos is viewed as emotional manipulation and will be treated with appropriate passive-aggression.

§14.5 – METRICS ROUNDING AND WEEKLY TOTALS INTEGRITY ACT

14.5.1 Acceptable rounding practices:

DISTANCE: 98.5 km → "100 km" ✅

TIME: 3:58 → "4 hours" ✅

ELEVATION: 985m → "1,000m" ✅

UNACCEPTABLE ROUNDING PRACTICES:

92 km → "Century" ✖

2:41 → "Nearly 3 hours" ✖

652m → "Alpine" ✗

14.5.2 Weekly totals must exclude:

- Dog walking,

- Errand commutes under 3 km,

- Golf,

- Recovery spins under 100 bpm (unless post-viral, and medically approved),

- Ice skating with toddlers.

14.5.3 Padding one's weekly mileage using the "record everything" tactic shall trigger an audit by peers, beginning with polite mockery and escalating to **CCS 5: BANTER BLACKOUT**.

§14.6 – DEBRIEF PROCEDURES AND COMMUNICATION STANDARDS

14.6.1 Post-ride discussion may occur via the following authorised channels:
(a) WhatsApp message ≤30 words,
(b) Memes with relevant caption,
(c) A single photo of cake or group camaraderie.

14.6.2 Voice notes exceeding 30 seconds without request or warning shall be treated as Broadcast Violations and met with social silence or counter-memeing.

14.6.3 The phrase "Still buzzing" is permitted. The phrase "Processing a lot from today's ride" is not–unless followed by professional follow-up counselling.

§14.7 – VISUAL MEDIA CONTROL AND IMAGE UPLOAD LAW

14.7.1 Photos may be uploaded, but shall be:

- Relevant,
- Few (≤3),
- Free of nasal intrusions or unnecessarily artistic flourishes.

14.7.2 The following are prohibited unless exceptional:

- Close-ups of cleats,
- GPS screen selfies,
- Gratuitous sweat shots,
- Locals.

14.7.3 Riders using multiple filters, vignettes, or excessive hashtags shall be referred to The Department of Aesthetic Restraint (DAR).

CHAPTER 15: EVENT DAY STATUTES FOR SPORTIVES, CLUB CHALLENGES, AND THE LIKE

And the cyclists gathered, clad in numbers and layered in ambition. And some did ride steady. And some did chat. And some—despite all their denials—did race.

§15.1 – THE DECLARATION OF INTENT TRANSPARENCY ACT

15.1.1 All riders participating in sportives, charity rides, or club-organised events must declare their intent honestly or remain silent.
– Acceptable pre-ride declarations:
(a) "Just aiming to get round,"
(b) "Steady day out,"
(c) "Let's enjoy it,"
(d) [No comment – legally safest].

15.1.2 Riders uttering "I'm just here for the views" and then riding threshold from the car park shall be issued CCS 3: Café Tax, and barred from future claim of ambivalence.

15.1.3 Riders stating "I'm not racing it" and then sprinting for every town sign shall be listed as Category X: Quietly Competing.

§15.2 – EQUIPMENT DISCLOSURE

15.2.1 Riders attending non-competitive events shall not bring:
(a) Disc wheelsets,
(b) Aero road helmets,
(c) Anything described as "pre-production prototype."

– Clause 15.2.1a: Use of such items while saying "It's just for comfort" shall be met with silence and slow head tilts.

15.2.2 Anyone calibrating a power meter in the car park while claiming to be "taking it easy" will be issued a **CCS 2: GROUP REMINDER**, accompanied by a sarcastic question about tyre pressure.

§15.3 – BEHAVIOURAL REGULATION DURING GROUP DEPARTURES

15.3.1 Neutral zones are to be respected. No surging, overlapping, or passive-aggressive rolling turns.
– Clause 15.3.1a: Riders accelerating off the front during the group photo shall be named in the minutes of the post-event roast.

15.3.2 All club events using the term "challenge" must be interpreted as:

"You may go hard, but you may not be a tool."
– Violators who half-wheel up climbs during "social waves" shall be placed at the back and monitored.

§15.4 – FEED STATION CONDUCT & EFFICIENCY EXPECTATIONS

15.4.1 Riders must choose their approach:
(a) Social grazers: Stop, sip, sample, selfie.
(b) Efficient functionals: Bottle refill, gel reload, gone.
(c) Shameful skippers: No stop, but tell everyone later they "meant to."

15.4.2 Judgement shall not be passed on the number of fig rolls consumed, unless hoarding occurs or custard creams are weaponised.

15.4.3 Riders who attend feed stations only for Instagram documentation and then complain about "dry banana bread" shall be banned from feedback surveys.

§15.5 – FINISH LINE DECLARATIONS AND MEMORY EDITING

15.5.1 Upon completion of the event, riders must not:
(a) Downplay their time while checking it obsessively,
(b) Refer to it as a "steady day out" if heart rate data proves otherwise,
(c) Upload it to Strava as "Recovery spin" if over 2,000 kcal burned.

15.5.2 Riders may say "That was lovely," "That hurt more than expected," or "I'm ready for cake."
– Clause 15.5.2a: Any reference to "zones" in the café line shall be met with **CCS 1: THE GLANCE**, unless coaching is your literal job.

§15.6 – INCLUSION AND CLUB CULTURE CLAUSE

15.6.1 All club event participants shall encourage newer riders, including:

- Explaining signage,
- Clarifying etiquette,
- Refraining from cornering at race speed into feed stops.

15.6.2 Riders who "accidentally" form a chain gang mid-sportive and drop everyone by the second feed stop must offer no apology—but must offer coffee.

15.6.3 No participant shall claim a solo moral victory unless they genuinely rode the route alone and weren't just dropped early.

§15.7 – AFTERMATH, UPLOADS & THE GREAT DEBRIEF

15.7.1 Event uploads shall follow the formatting set in §15. Titles must not include:

"Wasn't racing" (unless your average was <22 km/h),

"Just taking it easy" (if cadence never dropped below 90),

"First one back" (unless there is a published finish list to prove it).

15.7.2 Club event debriefs shall occur:

- In the group chat,
- Over cake,
- Or under breath in the car park.

– Voice notes exceeding 45 seconds must be cleared by the group's Communications Moderator.

§15.8 – CROSS-BORDER CLAUSES AND INTERNATIONAL INCIDENTS

15.8.1 Riders attending national or overseas trips must:
(a) Possess a valid passport (and not realise it's expired at the airport),
(b) Check baggage for energy gels with the diligence of MI5,
(c) Avoid announcing "I probably won't drink" before

a four-hour hotel bar session.

15.8.2 Training days on holiday are still training days. Showing up late because of wine, cheese, or Tinder shall not excuse missed intervals.

15.8.3 When mingling with locals, riders must:

(a) Attempt the local language (badly),

(b) Show appreciation for every coffee, pastry, and weird pork dish,

(c) Never comment on someone's saddle height unless asked.

15.8.4 Cultural offences include but are not limited to:

- Calling it a "foreign sportive,"

- Wearing pro team kit with flip flops,

- Referring to any road section as "basically Flanders."

15.8.5 Diplomatic immunity may be granted for poor conduct if rider buys a round and promises to upload only one photo with "suffering face."

CHAPTER 16: INFRACTIONS, SANCTIONS, AND THE ROLE OF THE GROUP RIDE ARBITRATOR

And lo, transgressions were committed. Some subtle, some egregious. And the bunch did murmur, then glare, then judge. And it was decided that justice must be dispensed—not by wrath, but by sarcastic consensus.

§16.1.0 – CATEGORIES OF OFFENCE

16.1.1 Infractions committed during group rides shall be classified into three tiers:

(a) Immediate – requiring on-the-road intervention (e.g. half-wheeling, signal failure, caffeinated arrogance)

(b) Deferred – judged post-ride at the café, in the WhatsApp group, or during the long descent of social opinion

(c) Compounded – where the offender is blissfully unaware until a pattern emerges and punishment is swift, brutal, and oddly polite

16.1.2 All infractions shall be graded according to the **Cyclist Citation Scale (CCS)**, from **CCS 1: THE GLANCE** to **CCS 6: THE EJECTION**

– Clause 16.1.2.1: **CCS 7: EXTERNAL ESCALATION** shall remain theoretical, unless civil infrastructure or horses are involved (see Chapter 8a)

§16.2.0 – THE ROLE AND AUTHORITY OF THE RIDE CAPTAIN

16.2.1 The Ride Captain (whether self-appointed or democratically shamed into it) shall have the power to:

• Issue on-the-spot **CCS 1–3** citations
• Demand formation compliance
• Broker peace between wheelsuckers and tempo pushers

16.2.2 The Ride Captain may not:

• Physically reposition riders
• Shout like a Tour commissaire

• Invent new rules mid-ride unless preceded by the phrase "Alright, hear me out…"

16.2.3 Resistance to the Ride Captain shall be met with **CCS 2: GROUP REMINDER**, and likely reassignment to backmarker purgatory

§16.3.0 – GROUP ARBITRATION AND POST-RIDE TRIALS

16.3.1 The group may convene an informal Rider Conduct Tribunal post-ride to discuss:
• Repeated misdemeanours
• Debrief-worthy etiquette breakdowns
• Violations of sock height or audible tubeless leakage

16.3.2 Tribunals shall be held at:
• The café table
• The WhatsApp group
• Quiet sections of recovery rides
– Verdicts are reached via sarcastic majority

16.3.3 Defendants may not defend themselves with:
"I didn't realise"
"That's how I always ride"
"My friend said it was fine"
– However, expressions of contrition accompanied by coffee and pastries shall be taken into account

§16.4.0 – PASSIVE SANCTION MEASURES

16.4.1 Where direct confrontation is deemed excessive, the following Passive Sanctions are authorised:
• The Silent Drop – accelerating subtly until the offender notices they are alone
• The Rear Reassignment – gently filtering the rider to

the back where no one talks

• The Muted Chat – temporary exclusion from digital banter for 24 hours

16.4.2 **CCS 5: BANTER BLACKOUT** may be triggered by:

• Egregious misuse of group chat
• Bragging uploads
• "I could've gone harder" post-ride declarations

§16.5.0 – REDEMPTION PATHWAYS

16.5.1 Riders may expunge one **CCS 1-3** offence by:

• Buying coffee for the group
• Pulling the group for 10 km into a headwind
• Publicly admitting guilt in the chat and promising better

16.5.2 Repeated offences shall result in **CCS 6: THE EJECTION** – a probationary ban from group rides until the next full moon or club social

16.5.3 Riders earning **CCS 6: THE EJECTION** must apply for re-entry by submitting:

(a) A written apology
(b) Demonstration of rule comprehension
(c) Photographic evidence of drivetrain maintenance

§16.6.0 – THE WITNESS CLAUSE

16.6.1 A minimum of two witnesses (or one rider with GoPro footage) is required for any sanction above **CCS 4**

– Anonymous accusations will be entertained only if:

(a) They're funny
(b) They're credible
(c) They're shared over flat whites

16.6.2 Riders falsely accusing others shall be subject to reverse citation and a week of leading solo recovery rides

§16.7.0 - THE FINAL AUTHORITY OF THE GROUP MOOD
16.7.1 Ultimately, enforcement of etiquette rests with the highest court in cycling: *The Vibe*
If the vibe is off, sanctions are justified. If the vibe is on, almost anything can be forgiven (except no mudguards in winter)
16.7.2 No rule shall override the shared, unspoken agreement that everyone is there to ride, survive, and return slightly better than they left—
and that no one likes the guy who takes all this too seriously

APPENDIX A: THE LEXICON OF THE ROAD – TRANSLATIONS, EUPHEMISMS, AND SUBTLE INSULTS DECODED

And they spake in tongues of cadence and code, where words meant not what they said, and praise was insult, and silence was thunder. Herein lies the translation of utterances heard upon the tarmac, for the protection of the naïve and the amusement of the fluent.

§A.1 – COMMON PHRASES AND THEIR TRUE MEANING

"JUST STEADY TODAY."
Translation: *I'm going to surge unexpectedly and pretend I didn't notice.*

"LET'S KEEP IT SOCIAL."
Translation: *Until I get bored or near a segment.*

"YOU GO AHEAD."
Translation: *I'm blown. If I chase, I'll see colours.*

"I'M JUST TAPPING IT OUT."
Translation: *I am absolutely burying myself and need you to think I'm holding back.*

"THAT CLIMB WAS OK."
Translation: *I just set a personal best and may cry at the café.*

"LEGS AREN'T THERE TODAY."
Translation: *I am still faster than you. Just setting expectations.*

"THIS IS MY RECOVERY RIDE."
Translation: *I plan to drop at least two people before coffee.*

"WE WAITED FOR YOU!"
Translation: *We slowed for 45 seconds while taking a gel.*

"YOU'RE RIDING WELL TODAY."
Translation: *I'm surprised and slightly offended you're still here.*

"ONLY A LITTLE KICKER AHEAD."

Translation: *The next 400m is 14%. Bring your lungs and a will.*

§A.2 - EUPHEMISMS FOR PHYSICAL COLLAPSE

"JUST GOING TO SPIN FOR A BIT."

Translation: *Zone 1 survival mode engaged.*

"I'LL SIT IN FOR A WHILE."

Translation: *The lights are on but nobody's home.*

"JUST FUELLING."

Translation: *I'm eating aggressively to hide my suffering.*

"DROPPED A BOTTLE BACK THERE."

Translation: *I dropped my ego and my glycogen.*

"I'M SAVING MYSELF FOR LATER."

Translation: *There is no later.*

§A.3 - TACTICAL SPEECH ON GROUP RIDES

"GROUP'S MOVING WELL."

Translation: *I'd like to slow down, but with dignity.*

"NICE PULL."

Translation: *That was suicidal. Please never do that again.*

"YOU'RE GOOD ON THE HILLS."

Translation: *Stop climbing like that. It's annoying.*

"TAKE YOUR TIME."

Translation: *Everyone's judging you but I'm pretending not to.*

"FLAT AFTER THIS."
Translation: *One more hill. Maybe two. Definitely pain.*

§A.4 – POST-RIDE PHRASES & THEIR SUBTEXT

"THAT WAS FUN."
Translation: *I'm traumatised but I won't show it.*

"GOOD RIDE, ALL."
Translation: *I hated that but will act gracious.*

"LET'S DO IT AGAIN SOON."
Translation: *You'll never see me again.*

"I FORGOT TO START MY COMPUTER."
Translation: *I need a do-over. This doesn't count.*

"I DIDN'T REALLY PUSH TODAY."
Translation: *I pushed. I cracked. I'm rebranding it.*

§A.5 – ADVANCED SARCASM INDICATORS

SILENCE AFTER A CLIMB.
Translation: *We are recalibrating social status.*

HEAVY BREATHING FOLLOWED BY "WELL DONE."
Translation: *You shouldn't have done that, but respect.*

"NICE SOCKS."
Translation: *You've breached several protocols (see Chapter 15).*

"INTERESTING BIKE CHOICE."
Translation: *I would never ride that, but I'm being polite.*

"DID YOU TRAIN MUCH THIS WEEK?"

Translation: *You're going too fast and I'm trying to destabilise you emotionally.*

§A.6 – CLOSING PROVERB

Trust not what is said, but how it is said, and always listen for what is not said. For on the group ride, words are watts in disguise.

APPENDIX B: ADDED PERNICKETYNESS REGARDING SOCKS – REGULATION, REPRESENTATION, AND THE LIMITS OF LYCRA LIBERTY

And lo, there was sock. And it was visible. And it was judged.

§B.1 – THE CODIFIED SOCK HEIGHT RANGE (CSHR)

B.1.1 The Zone of Acceptable Sock Height (ZASH) is defined as:

- No lower than 2 cm above the ankle bone,
- No higher than the base of the calf.

– Anything outside these bounds shall be deemed either Insubstantial (ankle-baring) or Unholy (calf-hugging) and is subject to **CCS 2: GROUP REMINDER**.

– Sympathy is extended to those with modestly proportioned calves, for whom the "base" is a philosophical concept rather than a visible landmark. In these cases, intent and effort will be considered mitigating factors.

B.1.2 Height violations of more than 3 cm shall result in **CCS 3: CAFÉ TAX**, payable in pastry.

B.1.3 Height asymmetry (difference in sock elevation between legs) must not exceed 1.5 CM, except in cases of declared injury, post-wash shrinkage, or theatrical intent.

§B.2 – COLOURATION AND THEMATIC CONSISTENCY DOCTRINE

B.2.1 WHITE SOCKS are recognised as the international default during dry months. They imply intent, discipline, and moderate emotional stability.
– *Clause B.2.1a:* Dirty white socks are WORSE THAN NO SOCKS and shall trigger **CCS 4: TRIBUNAL** under the Aesthetic Negligence Clause.

B.2.2 BLACK SOCKS are legally admissible in conditions of inclement weather, off-season training, or when paired with a monochrome kit of sufficient composure.

B.2.3 NEON SOCKS are permitted under the following exemptions:
(a) You are a commuter,
(b) You are intentionally ironic,
(c) You hit your teens in the 80s.

B.2.4 Patterned or novelty socks must:

- Be symmetrical,

- Coordinate with no more than one additional item of kit,

- Contain no visible slogans, memes, or food groups.

– Violations incur **CCS 2**, unless accompanied by exceptional climbing ability.

§B.3 – MATERIAL, CONDITION, AND LIFECYCLE MANAGEMENT

B.3.1 All socks must be:

- Purpose-built for cycling,

- Moisture-wicking,

- Free of holes, bobbles, or post-wash trauma.

B.3.2 **COMPRESSION SOCKS** are permitted under declaration of medical need, ageing quads, or mid-season crisis.

– Clause B.3.2a: They must not be worn with ankle bands, cargo bibs, or ego.

B.3.3 Socks with frayed cuffs, faded branding, or formerly-white-now-beige colourways shall be respectfully retired.

§B.4 – THE OVERSHOE OBFUSCATION EXEMPTION

B.4.1 In winter conditions (<10°C), socks may be concealed by overshoes or toe thingys. However, riders must still observe the spirit of sock conduct.
– Clause B.4.1a: Bright-coloured socks bursting forth from the tops of overshoes must be intentional or explained.

B.4.2 Mid-ride sock reveals—removing overshoes to expose crimes against hosiery—shall be treated as a violation of latent sock protocol, with penalties backdated.

§B.5 – SOCK AUDIT PROCEDURES

B.5.1 Any rider may call a Sock Audit at a café stop or pre-ride muster, provided:
(a) They are wearing compliant socks themselves,
(b) They do not abuse the audit for personal amusement,
(c) They carry the appropriate tone of dry authority.

B.5.2 Failed audits result in:

- Public notification,

- One-week probation,

- A group recommendation to "sort it out."

§B.6 – SYMBOLIC WEIGHT OF SOCKS CLAUSE

B.6.1 Socks represent:

- Your level of effort,

- Your intent,

- Your silent understanding of the Codex.

B.6.2 In moments of doubt, let the sock speak for you.
If it whispers, "I care, but not too much," you have succeeded.
If it screams, "LOOK AT ME," you have failed.
If it disappears entirely, go home and start again.

APPENDIX C: THE FINAL BENEDICTION OF THE ROAD – CLOSING THE BOOK OF CYCLING LAW

And when the last climb was crested, and the final flat white consumed, there remained only wisdom—written not in stone, but in sweat, sarcasm, and tyre tracks.

§C.1 – The Spirit of the Peloton

C.1.1 These laws, guidelines, and rituals exist not to constrain, but to elevate.
Not to ridicule, but to remind:

That cycling is joy disguised as discipline,
Camaraderie wrapped in Lycra,
And occasionally, a passive-aggressive tempo surge.

C.1.2 To ride well is not merely to pedal fast, but to pull when it matters, sit in when it's kind, signal when it's safe, and know that good etiquette is the lubricant of the group ride—not chain lube (though that matters too).

§.2 – In Memory of the Fallen Protocols

C.2.1 Let us remember those who:

- Rode without mudguards in February,
- Half-wheeled their own friends,
- Uploaded "just a spin" at 40 km/h.
- Undertook a full interval session unannounced in the middle of a social ride, leaping off the front, falling back in recovery.

They taught us what not to do, and for that, we thank them.

§C.3 – Revision and Local Amendments

C.3.1 This codex is living. It may be adapted by clubs, crews, and cults, provided:

Amendments are made in the same tone,

Disputes are settled with humour or cake,

No rule ever excuses being a dick.

C.3.2 Should contradictions arise, local custom prevails unless the custom is clearly ridiculous, in which case universal judgement applies.

§C.4 – THE FINAL CLAUSE

C.4.1 You may ride solo.
You may race.
You may simply pootle and admire the sheep.
But once you ride in a group,

You enter into a sacred contract.
Not written.
But now... written.

Read it. Know it. Uphold it.
Or at the very least, don't half-wheel.